Explorations

Contents

Europe and the East

Europe and the world in 1400

About six hundred years ago people did not
know much about the lands and seas of the world.
People living in one land did not even know that
some of the other lands existed.

This map shows you what the people living in Europe
thought the world looked like.

A map of the world which was made in Europe
in about 1406. It is a copy of one made by a
Greek called Ptolemy who lived in Alexandria,
in Egypt, just over 1,800 years ago.

People thought the world was three parts land and one part water. They thought the land was divided into three big areas called Europe, Africa and Asia. Find these on the map.

They also believed there was a fourth great land in the south that they had not discovered yet. Find it on the map. It is shown at the bottom joining Africa to Asia.

Some people thought strange beasts and monsters lived there. These are drawings of them from another map which was made in the thirteenth century.

The map below shows you what we know today about the lands and seas of the world. Use the two maps to work out which parts of the world people living in Europe six hundred years ago did not know about.

A map of the world today. Find:
● **North America**
● **South America**
● **Australia**
● **New Zealand.**
Now look at the map of 1406.
Can you find them on it?

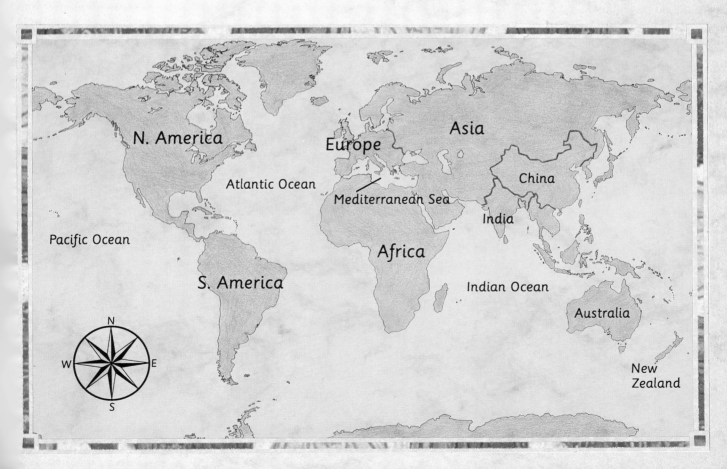

The wealth of the East

There was one part of the world that most interested European people six hundred years ago. It was the eastern part of Asia, which they called the East. They believed it was a strange and mysterious land, full of great riches.

Some people knew of the Italian explorer, Marco Polo, who had travelled over land to Cathay, which we call China, in 1271.

A fourteenth-century Chinese painting of Quinsay (modern Hangchow), the capital city of Cathay, which Marco Polo visited.

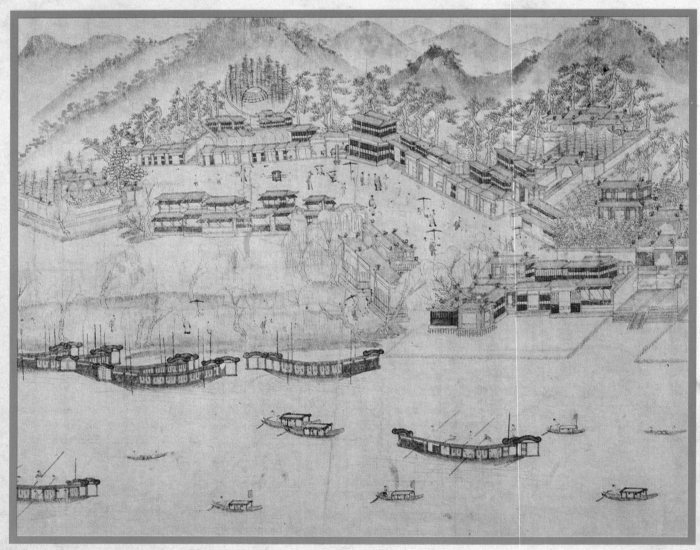

Marco Polo wrote a book about his travels. He told of the Grand Khan, the powerful ruler of Cathay, and of his marble palaces.

He described a great sea-port, called Zaitun, where ships arrived from India, another of the rich lands in the East. He said they were full of precious stones, enormous pearls and valuable **spices**. He said some of the spices came from islands in the East. He called them the Spice Islands. Today we call them the 'Moluccas'.

Spices

Spices are used in cooking to give special flavours to food. They come from certain plants which have a very strong taste.

Spices

Six hundred years ago people did not know how to keep food fresh for very long. Spices were very important because they made food that was going bad seem more pleasant to eat. Some spices even helped food to stay fresh for longer than usual.

Poor people in Europe used herbs and spices they could grow or find for themselves, such as thyme, mint, aniseed and garlic. But rich people wanted the spices that came from the East such as pepper, cloves, cinnamon, nutmeg and ginger.

In those days people also used the word 'spice' to mean **perfume** and **incense**. These came from the East too.

Ginger

Spices are still used a lot today because people enjoy the taste. Which ones do you have at home?

Cloves

Perfume

A liquid with a sweet smell, or scent. It is often made from flowers.

Cinnamon

Nutmeg and Mace

Pepper

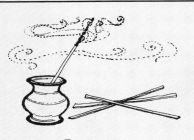

Incense

Spices and gums which give off a sweet smell when they are burned.

5

Trade between East and West

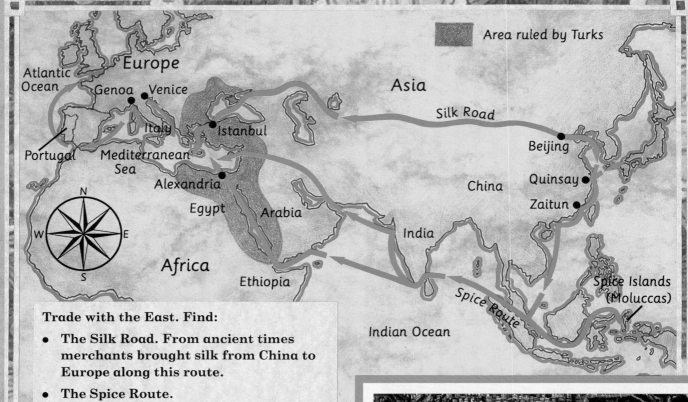

Trade with the East. Find:

- The Silk Road. From ancient times merchants brought silk from China to Europe along this route.
- The Spice Route.

Only rich Europeans could afford the spices, silks and precious stones that came from the East. These things were very expensive because merchants had to carry them such a long way. Find their routes on the map.

Now find the lands ruled by the Turks. The Turks were **Muslims**. They stopped merchants from Europe, who were **Christians**, from travelling to the East through their lands.

Muslim merchants brought goods from the East to Alexandria, Antioch and Istanbul. There they were bought by merchants from Italian cities such as Genoa and Venice. They took them away in huge ships called galleys and sold them in Europe. Find these places on the map.

This is Genoa painted about five hundred years ago. The people living there could afford to put up splendid buildings.

Muslims	Christians
People who follow the religion of Islam. They believe in the life and teachings of the Prophet Mohammed.	People who follow the religion of Christianity. They believe in the life and teachings of Jesus Christ.

Prince Henry of Portugal

Merchants in other European countries were angry with the Italians because they would not share the trade from the East. They were also angry with the Turks for stopping them from travelling to the East. Why do you think the Turks wanted to stop them?

This is Prince Henry of Portugal. He wanted to fight the Turks and give the spice trade to the Christians. He believed an old story that said a powerful Christian king, called Prester John, lived in the East. We now know the story was not true, but Prince Henry did not know that.

Prince Henry believed Prester John lived in Ethiopia in East Africa. Find it on the map. He wanted to find Prester John to ask him to help fight the Turks.

Now find Portugal on the map. Prince Henry's plan was to send sailors from there to explore the west coast of Africa to see if there was a way round to Ethiopia.

Henry paid for the best sailors, ship-builders and map-makers to help him. Their first job was to invent a ship good enough for explorers to use.

Prester John, the imaginary king of Ethiopia.
This picture comes from an old map.

Ships and Navigation

Ships

This picture is of a king sailing in a ship
nine hundred years ago, in about 1100.
It is very like the ones the Vikings used.

Find:

- the rudder, shaped like an oar, on one side.
- the holes along the side for oars.
- the sail.
- the carved wooden head at the front.

The ships in 1400 were much bigger and stronger than the ones used three hundred years before, but they were difficult to sail in rough seas. It took a long time for them to change direction, so they were no use for exploring unknown seas.

This is a model of a ship used six hundred years ago, in about 1400.

The model is five hundred years old. It was made in Holland. Find:

- **the mast**
- **the look-out place at the top of the mast.**
This is called a 'crow's nest'. Can you work out why?
- **the ropes and pulleys.**
- **the sail**
- **the platforms at the front and back.**

The back of the model.

Find the rudder. What are the differences between this ship and the one on page 8? Is anything the same?

Prince Henry of Portugal had to start by building a ship which would sail round Africa.

Portuguese sailors already used very small ships called 'caravels'. They usually had one or two masts and triangular sails, called 'lateen' sails.

Henry's ship-builders invented bigger caravels like this one. They were large enough to carry all the stores for a long journey and strong enough to stand up to stormy weather and rough seas.

Later they decided to mix lateen sails, which were best for sailing into the wind, with square sails, which were best when the wind was behind the ship. They also put two sails on the main mast instead of one.

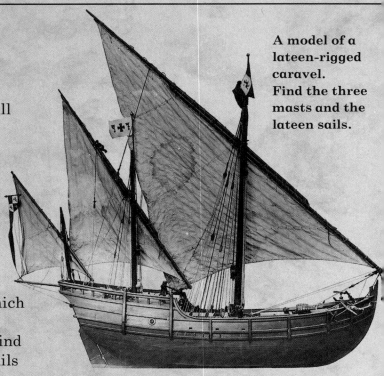

A model of a lateen-rigged caravel.
Find the three masts and the lateen sails.

For the next hundred and fifty years sailors tried out different arrangements of square and lateen sails, and main and top-sails.

This painting shows Portuguese ships called 'carracks', which were bigger than caravels, in about 1550.

- How many masts do these ships have?
- How many sails?
- Which are square and which lateen?
- What is the difference between one of these carracks and a caravel?
- Is anything the same?
- Find the members of the ships' crews.
- What are they doing?

A model of a square-rigged caravel. Find:

● the large square sails

● the smaller square top-sail

● the lateen sail.

Rigged

How a ship is rigged is the way its masts and sails are arranged.
A lateen-rigged ship is one that has mainly triangular sails.
A square-rigged ship has mainly square sails.

Navigation

Sailors usually liked to stay near the coast so that they knew where they were. So how did the explorers **navigate** when they were in unknown seas, miles from land?

They could find out the direction they were sailing in by looking at the stars. As long as they were north of the **equator** they could see this pattern of stars called the 'Plough'. It pointed to a bright star called the 'Pole Star' which they knew always lay in the north.

The lines on the picture have been drawn to help you find the pattern the stars make.

Why do you think this pattern of stars is called the Plough?
See if you can find the Plough and the Pole Star on a clear night.

Navigate

To work out the right course to follow and steer the ship on it.

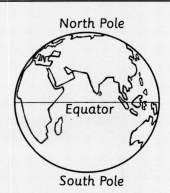

Equator

An imaginary line that circles the earth exactly half-way between the north and the south poles.

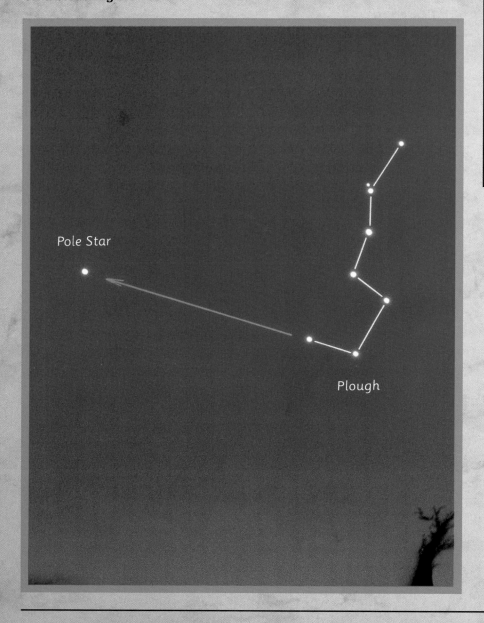

Pole Star

Plough

When explorers crossed the equator going south, they found they could see a new group of stars which they called the 'Southern Cross'. The bottom of the cross always pointed to the south.

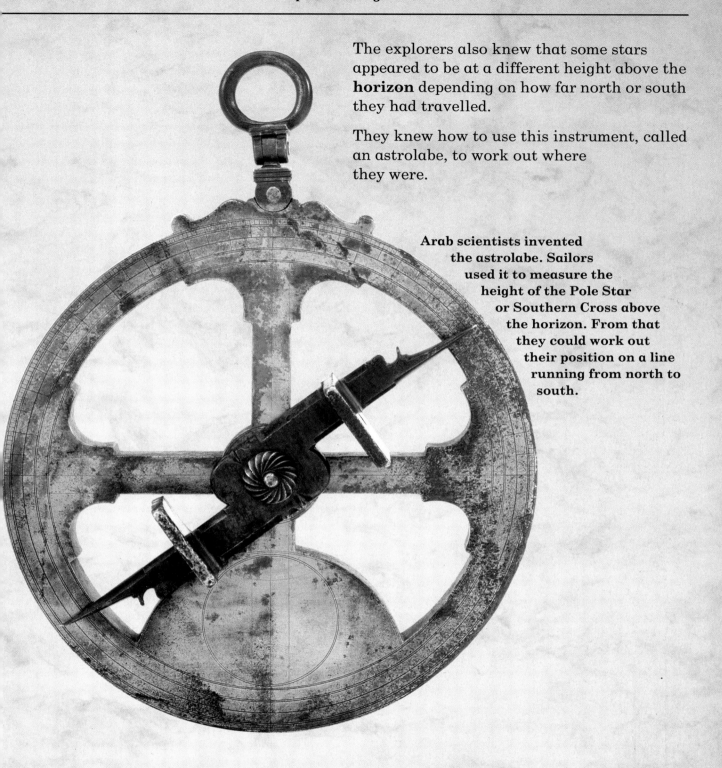

The explorers also knew that some stars appeared to be at a different height above the **horizon** depending on how far north or south they had travelled.

They knew how to use this instrument, called an astrolabe, to work out where they were.

Arab scientists invented the astrolabe. Sailors used it to measure the height of the Pole Star or Southern Cross above the horizon. From that they could work out their position on a line running from north to south.

It was difficult to use an astrolabe on board a ship rolling in the waves, so they had to find land before they could use it properly.

Horizon

The line where the sky appears to meet land or sea.

The **pilot** of one of Henry's ships had some simple instruments to help him navigate.

He had a compass to tell him in which direction he was sailing.

Pilot

A sailor with the special skill of navigating.

This compass was made in about 1580. The needle is a magnet which always points to the north. It is fixed to a card marked with compass points.
The card is fixed on a pin so that it can spin round.
On board ship the compass was put inside a box fixed to the deck.
An oil lamp lit up the card at night.

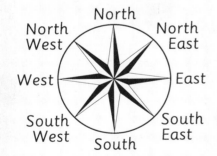

Compass points

The four main points of the compass are north, south, east and west.
The points between them are north-east, south-east, south-west and north-west.
There are thirty-two compass points altogether.

He had an hour-glass to tell him how long he had been sailing in that direction.

An hour-glass.
It worked like a modern egg-timer. The sand took half an hour to run from top to bottom. Then you turned the glass over so that the sand could run back the other way.

The pilot worked out how fast the ship was moving by watching the speed of bubbles or bits of seaweed which floated past.

If he multiplied the speed of the ship by the time he had been travelling, he knew how far he had gone in one direction. Then he used a ruler and a pair of dividers to mark the ship's course, and its new position, on a **chart**.

Henry told his map-makers to use the information the pilots brought back to make charts like this of the seas they had explored.

Chart
A map of the sea.

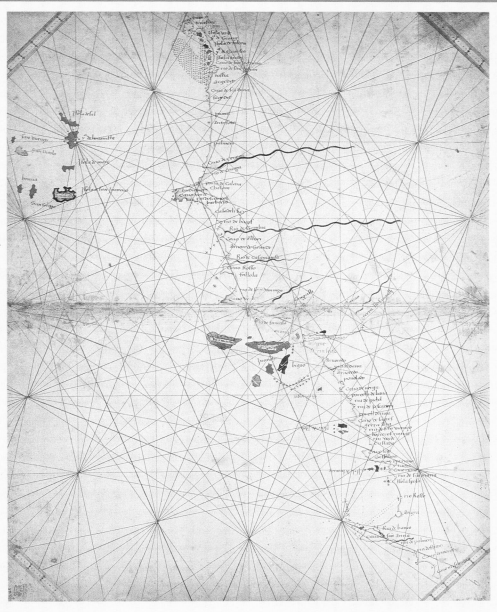

A chart of the west coast of Africa and part of the Atlantic Ocean, made by the Portuguese in 1463.

Find:

- the African coast
- islands
- the lines meeting at different points. They helped sailors to work out which point of the compass to sail along to get to a particular place.

Explorers Sail East

The Portuguese and Africa

Here is a recent photograph of a market on the coast of West Afric today. It is probably not very different from the markets the Portuguese explorers found when they landed there for the first time about four hundred and fifty years ago.

Find:

● the things for sale. What are they?

● the sellers

● the buyers. How do they carry things?

What is the same in your local market? Is anything different?

Prince Henry sent explorers out from Portugal from about 1418 until his death in 1460. Look at the map. Find where they went. By about 1480 the Portuguese explorers had reached Benin. Find it on the map.

The Portuguese explorers did not find the way round Africa which Prince Henry was looking for, but they did find pepper and gold dust in the African markets.

They started to trade European goods in return for these. They also tried to capture African people to take home to sell as slaves. Sometimes they traded horses and cloth with merchants in return for slaves.

Portugese exploration between 1418 and 1480.

Azores

Portugal   Spain
● Lisbon
● Sagres

Madeira

Canary Islands

Africa

Cape Verde
Islands

Cape Verde
Gambia

Sierra Leone
Liberia   Benin

N
W   E
S

—— voyages of the
Portuguese explorers

places visited by the
Portuguese explorers

The people of Benin were clever artists.

This is a **bronze** sculpture made in Benin about five hundred years ago.

The sculpture shows a warrior on horseback. Find:

● **his head-dress**
● **his weapon**
● **the patterns on his clothes.**
● **the horse's harness.**

Bronze

A mixture of copper and tin.

17

Bartolomeo Dias and the Cape of Good Hope

In 1487 the Portuguese king, John, ordered Bartolomeo Dias to sail along the coast of Africa until he found the way to the Indian Ocean and the rich lands of India.

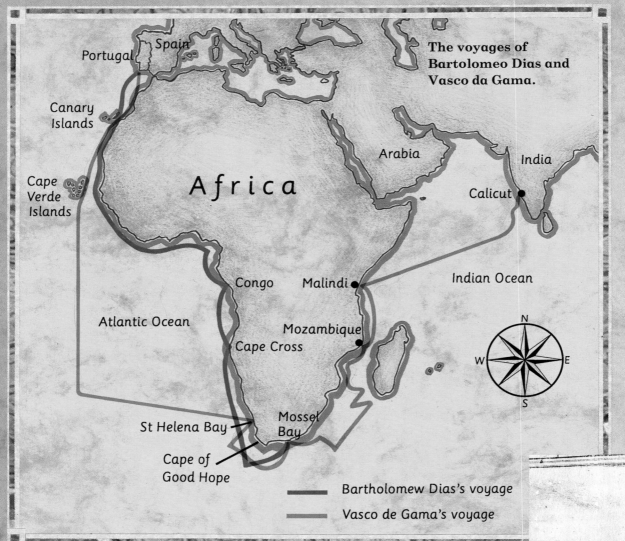

The voyages of Bartolomeo Dias and Vasco da Gama.

Portugal · Spain · Canary Islands · Cape Verde Islands · Africa · Arabia · India · Calicut · Congo · Malindi · Indian Ocean · Atlantic Ocean · Mozambique · Cape Cross · St Helena Bay · Mossel Bay · Cape of Good Hope

N W E S

—— Bartholomew Dias's voyage
—— Vasco de Gama's voyage

Follow his voyage on the map. First he sailed to Cape Cross. This was as far as explorers had been before. Then a storm blew him out of sight of land. It drove him south for thirteen days.

When the wind dropped, Dias turned towards the coast. After several days there was still no sign of land. Then he guessed what had happened. He had sailed round the southern end of Africa.

He steered north and reached Mossel Bay. Dias wanted to go on, but his men were worn out. Soon he turned for home.

Dias named the southern tip of Africa the 'Cape of Storms'. But King John changed this to the 'Cape of Good Hope' because now there was a chance of finding a way to India.

Vasco da Gama and India

This is Vasco da Gama. In 1497, Manuel, the new king of Portugal, ordered him to find the way from the Cape of Good Hope to India.

Follow da Gama's voyage on the map. First he sailed right out into the Atlantic Ocean. He was out of sight of land for ninety-six days. He landed at St Helena Bay.

Then he sailed round the Cape and followed the coast to Mozambique. He asked for a pilot to show him the way to India. But the people living there did not want to help him. In the end the ruler of Malindi agreed to lend him one.

The pilot took da Gama's ships to Calicut in India. They found spices and precious stones in the markets there. Some of the spices came from the Spice Islands.

After that, Manuel sent many more ships to India. He sent soldiers to guard the Portuguese merchants. Soon the Portuguese found the Spice Islands and managed to reach China.

This is the Indian port of Calicut.
Find:
- the ships. How many different sorts are there?

Which ones are probably Portuguese? How can you tell?
- the elephants.
- the ruler of Calicut.

CALECHVT CELEBERRI-
MVM INDIÆ EMPORIVM.

Life on Board the Ships

The crew of a ship had to put sails up and
take them down in all weathers.
To do this they had to climb up the masts using ropes
called 'rigging'. Then they had to go out on the 'yard',
the wooden bar that held the sail.
Imagine doing that when the ship was tossing in
the waves in stormy weather.

Find:
- the sailors in the crow's nest keeping a look-out.
- the sailors on the yard.

The explorers' ships were quite small, often with a crew of no more than twenty. Here are the people who sailed on a ship and the jobs they had to do.

	Job
Officers	
Captain	In charge of everybody on the ship. Made all the important decisions about where to sail and what to do.
Master	In charge of the sailors. Gave all the orders to do with actually sailing the ship.
Pilot	Second in charge of the sailors. In charge of navigating the ship, working out the right course and plotting it on a chart.
Surgeon	Looked after the sick and wounded. Not every ship had a special surgeon.
Boatswain	Leader of the sailors. In charge of making sure the sailors carried out the orders of the Master or the Pilot. Made sure the ship and its equipment was in good working order.
Steward	In charge of food, firewood for cooking, water and wine.
Crew	
Able Seamen	Carried out the orders of the Master or Pilot. Some of them had special skills such as carpenters and caulkers whose job was to stop up leaks in the ship.
Boys	Learning to be Able Seamen. One of them had to turn the hour glass every half hour.

We do not know of any women who sailed on board the explorers' ships.
Do you think that means they did not?

The crew were divided into two teams, called 'watches'. One watch was on 'watch', or duty, while the other was off. Most watches lasted four hours.

The sailors on duty after dawn had to scrub the decks. The next watch had to pump out the water that had washed on board overnight. It was collected in the bottom of the ship which was always very smelly indeed. If too much collected in the bottom, the weight of the water might have made the ship sink.

All through the day the sailors had to mend sails, ropes and pulleys and make sure everything worked properly.

This picture shows Spanish sailors setting sail in a caravel.

'Tiller' for steering

Rudder

Find:
- the men in the crow's nest.
- the men on the rigging.
- the sailor pulling up the mainsail.
- the man being sick over the side.
- the men drinking wine from clay bottles.
- the water barrel on deck.
- the drummer and fife-player at the back.

We know from descriptions people wrote at the time that this
is how a caravel probably looked inside.

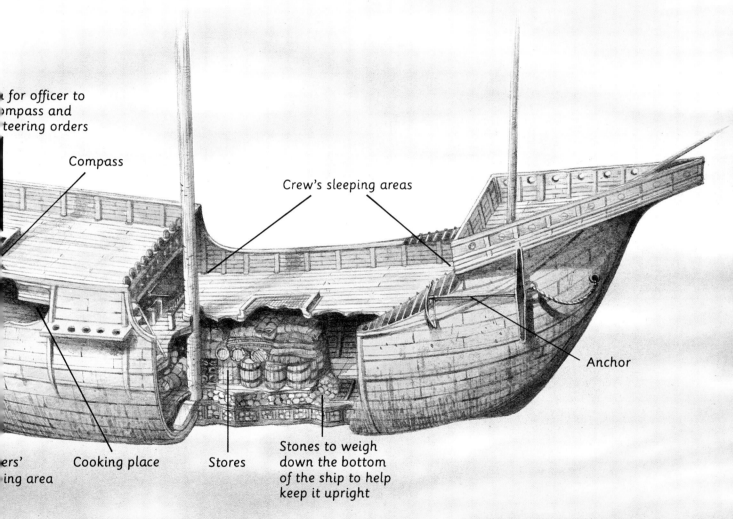

for officer to
ompass and
teering orders

Compass

Crew's sleeping areas

Anchor

ers'
ing area

Cooking place

Stores

Stones to weigh
down the bottom
of the ship to help
keep it upright

The crew had to find a place to sleep on deck. No one wanted to go down where the stores were kept because of the dark and smells. The officers often slept in the covered area near the rudder.

This was also where a fire was made for cooking. It was in a metal box with sand in the bottom. Why did the sailors have to be very careful with fire in a wooden ship?

The sailors ate biscuit, dried fish, salted beef or pork, and beans, peas and lentils. They caught fresh fish at sea. They took fresh water in barrels but it soon went stale. They also took wine in clay jars. Many of them died from a disease called scurvy because they could not eat enough fresh meat and vegetables on a long voyage.

Explorers Sail West

Christopher Columbus

Five hundred years ago an Italian sailor
called Christopher Columbus decided to try to
reach the East from Spain by sailing westwards,
straight across the Atlantic Ocean.
He believed this was possible because he thought the
world looked like this.

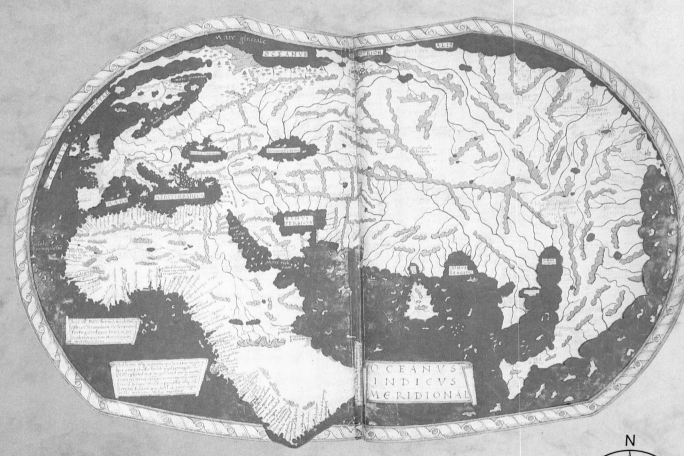

Henricus Martellus made this map in about 1489.
Find Africa. You can see that Martellus marked
places on the coast as far as Mossel Bay where
Bartolomeo Dias landed. America is missing
because at the time no one living in Europe
knew it was there.

Columbus was excited by Marco Polo's stories of the East and especially his description of the rich island of Cipangu which today we call Japan.

Sailors were frightened to sail out of sight of land into the Atlantic Ocean, which they called the Ocean Sea. Some thought that giant monsters lived there. Others believed stories that the world was flat and that they would sail off the edge.

Columbus was an experienced sailor. He had sailed in Portuguese ships north to Iceland and south to West Africa. Most people in those days knew the world was round, and he knew he would not sail off the edge. But no one knew how wide the Ocean Sea was.

This was important. If it was too wide explorers would run out of food before they reached Cipangu on the other side. Columbus tried to work it out. But he calculated that the world is smaller than it really is. Also, he did not know about America.

Christopher Columbus. This picture was painted long after he died. No one painted him when he was alive.

Columbus worked out that the world was like this.

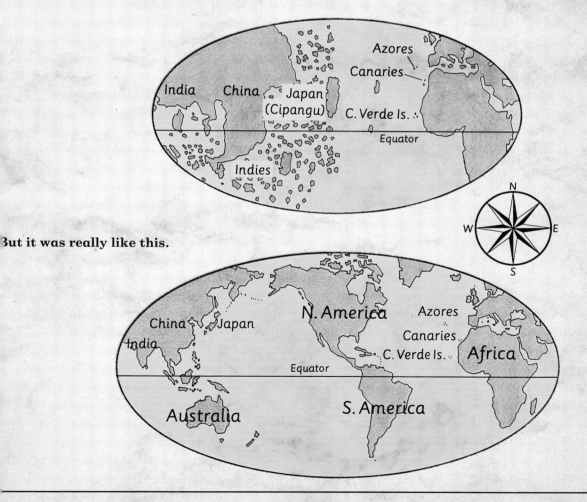

But it was really like this.

It took Columbus eight years to get anyone to give him money for ships and sailors. At last Queen Isabella and King Ferdinand of Spain decided to pay for his journey.

Now Columbus had to persuade people to take a risk and sail with him. He was helped by a man called Martin Pinzon and his two brothers. They told sailors they had a chance to make their fortunes. Ninety sailors agreed to go with them.

They set sail in 1492 in three ships called the 'Pinta', the 'Nina' and the 'Santa Maria'. These models show how they may have looked.

The 'Pinta', a square-rigged caravel.
She was about twenty-two metres long and seven-and-a-half wide. Martin Pinzon was her captain. She had a crew of twenty-six.

The 'Nina', a lateen-rigged caravel.
Later Columbus had her rig changed so that she looked like the 'Pinta'. She was about twenty two metres long and seven wide.
Martin Pinzon's brother, Vincente, was her captain. She had a crew of twenty-four.

The 'Santa Maria'.
She was a type of ship called a 'nao', fatter than a caravel and not so easy to sail. She was about twenty-five metres long and eight-and-a-half wide. Columbus made her the flagship and captained her himself. She had a crew of forty.

Flagship

The leading ship. The other ships knew where to go because they could see the flag on the flagship.

Look at the map. Columbus worked out that the winds in the Ocean Sea blow in opposite directions. He wanted to have the winds behind him on the way out to Cipangu. So he planned to start his crossing from the Canary Islands, rather than from Spain. He kept a diary on the voyage that tells us some of the things that happened.

The arrows show the direction of the winds. Columbus knew it would be very difficult to sail straight out into the Ocean Sea from Spain because the winds there blow against ships trying to go westwards. He planned to use those winds to take him home.

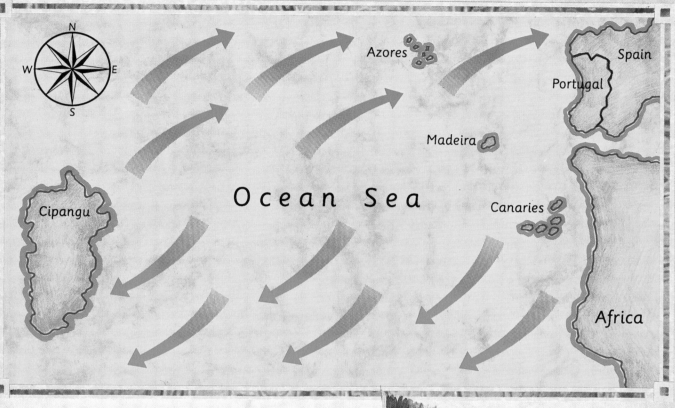

He was right about the wind. It blew his ships westwards from the Canary Islands for thirteen days. Then it dropped and the sea became calm. The ships hardly moved. They seemed to be stranded.

Then Martin Pinzon called out 'Land, Land!' Everyone was very excited. But it turned out to be a cloud on the horizon.

They had been out of sight of land for twenty days, longer than anyone else before them. Then the wind picked up again. They saw birds, seaweed and flying fish.

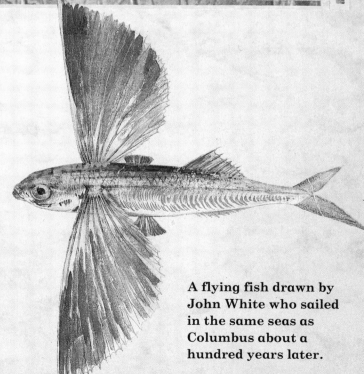

A flying fish drawn by John White who sailed in the same seas as Columbus about a hundred years later.

After thirty days, the sailors were very frightened. They wanted to turn back. Columbus and the Pinzon brothers persuaded them to keep going for a day or two longer.

The next night there was another shout of 'Land! Land!'. The lookout on 'Pinta' could see a line of cliffs ahead. This time there was no mistake. In the morning Columbus was rowed ashore. He had found an island.

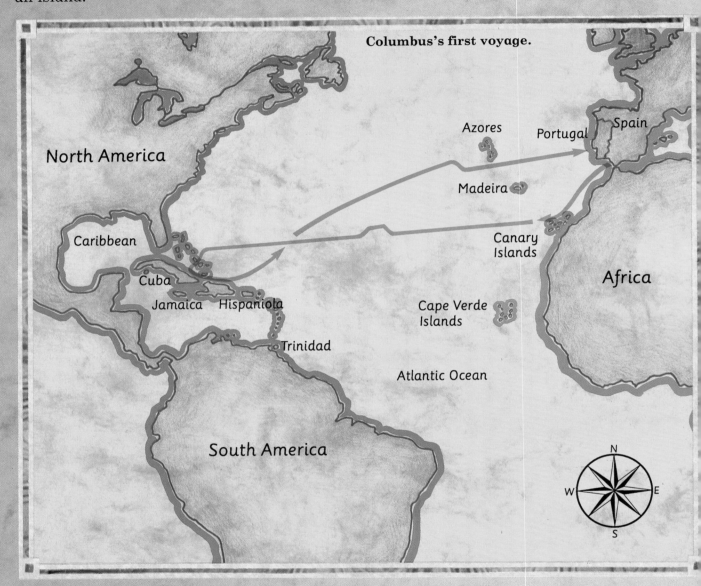

Columbus's first voyage.

In fact Columbus had reached the islands of the Caribbean. Find them on the map. The people who lived there were Caribs and Arawaks.

But Columbus was sure he had reached the East. He called the islands the 'Indies' and the people who lived there 'Indians'. He said the islands now belonged to Queen Isabella and King Ferdinand. What do you think the people who lived there thought about this?

He saw some 'Indians' wearing gold jewellery so he sailed round the islands trying to find gold mines.

This picture shows Columbus landing on one of the islands.
It was drawn by a European artist a hundred years afterwards.
How accurate do you think it is?
How might an Arawak artist have drawn the scene?

Find:
- the ships.
- Columbus holding a spear. This is the royal spear of Spain. Columbus said that all the islands now belonged to Isabella and Ferdinand.
- men putting up a cross. This is the Christian sign. The islanders had their own religious beliefs, but Columbus wanted them to become Christians. How do you think they felt about this?
- the Arawaks giving Columbus presents. Do you think they did this? What do you think the Arawaks behind them are supposed to be doing?

Then the 'Santa Maria' hit a rock and was wrecked. Columbus left thirty-eight of his men behind in a fort, and sailed home with the rest and some of the Arawaks in the other two ships.

He showed Queen Isabella and King Ferdinand the things he had brought back from the 'Indies' - some gold, plants, parrots, and hammocks which Europeans had never seen before.

Columbus was sure that one of the islands he had found was Cipangu. He made three more voyages to try to reach India. He still believed it was just west of the islands. He died in 1506, a disappointed man.

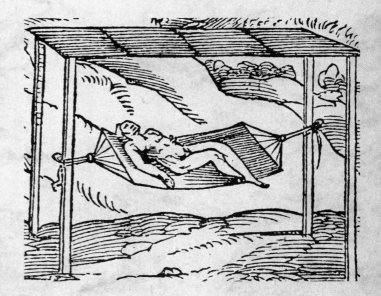

An Arawak using a hammock. European sailors thought that hammocks were such a good idea that they borrowed the invention and used them in ships instead of sleeping on the deck.

John Cabot

This is a model of a ship called the *Matthew*. In 1497 an Italian sailor called John Cabot set out in her from Bristol with his brother Sebastian and a crew of seventeen.

Cabot believed he could reach Asia by sailing across the northern part of the Ocean Sea. Then he would turn south and find the Spice Islands.

The crew of the *Matthew* were out of sight of land for fifty-four days. Then they reached the coast of Canada. Follow their journey on the map.

The voyage of the *Matthew*.

Cabot was sure he had reached Asia. He made the same mistake as Christopher Columbus. The next year he made another voyage. He hoped to find Cipangu and bring back spices and gold. But he returned to Bristol with nothing.

Cabot was not the first European to reach Canada. The Vikings sailed there about five hundred years before him, but their story had been forgotten. You can read about it in *Invasions!*

Ferdinand Magellan

This is a Portuguese captain called Ferdinand Magellan. In 1519 he set out from Spain with five ships to find a way round the southern tip of South America. After that he planned to sail on to the Spice Islands. The King of Spain wanted them to belong to Spain.

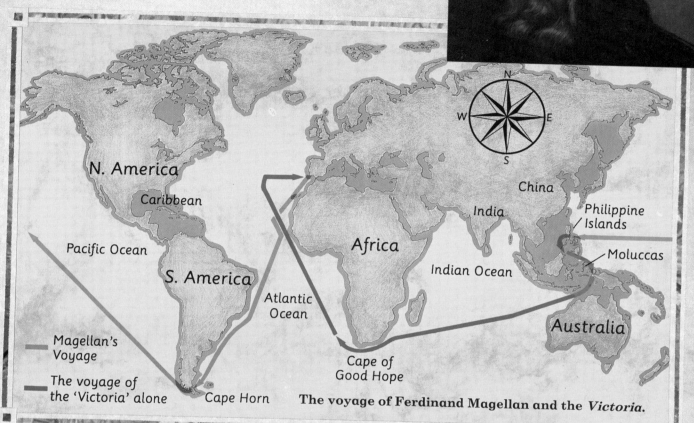

The voyage of Ferdinand Magellan and the *Victoria*.

Cape Horn is at the tip of South America. Find it on the map. Magellan did not try to sail round Cape Horn. He found a narrow channel through the islands that led to the Pacific Ocean.

By now Magellan had only three ships. One had been wrecked and the crew of another had decided to sail back home. After several months he reached the Philippine Islands. Find them on the map.

All the explorers from Europe wanted the islanders where they landed to become Christian like them. Magellan managed to persuade the chief of one of the Philippine islands to become a Christian. Why do you think the chief agreed?

Magellan was killed fighting some of the chief's enemies.

After that the crew sailed to the Spice Islands. From there one ship, the *Victoria*, sailed on westwards loaded with spices. She was the first ship to sail all the way round the world. It had taken three years.

The world in 1550

By 1550 Europeans knew much more about the world than their ancestors did a hundred and fifty years before.

This is Ptolemy's map which Europeans used in about 1400.

This is a map they used in about 1570.

A map-maker called Mercator drew this map in 1569.
What are the differences between this map and Ptolemy's map?
Is anything the same? Which lands that we know about today
are not on it?